PIONEERS IN WOMEN'S SPORTS

BY BRIAN HALL

WOMEN IN SPORTS

An Imprint of Abdo Publishing
abdopublishing.com

abdopublishing.com

Printed in the United States of America, North Mankato, Minnesota
042017
092017

Cover Photo: AP Images
Interior Photos: AP Images, 1, 9, 10–11, 14, 20–21, 36; Butch Comegys/The Times & Tribune/AP Images, 5; Chronos Dokumentarfilm GmbH/ullstein bild/Getty Images, 6; Press Association/AP Images, 13; Jason Heidrich/Icon Sportswire, 17; Columbia Pictures/Photofest NYC, 19; Transcendental Graphics/Getty Images, 23; Dilip Vishwanat/Duluth News-Tribune/AP Images, 24; Bettmann/Getty Images, 27; Harold Valentine/AP Images, 28; Tom Strattman/AP Images, 31; Kevork Djansezian/AP Images, 33; John G. Zimmerman/Sports Illustrated/Getty Images, 35; Matt York/AP Images, 39; Mark Duncan/AP Images, 41; Paul Jasienski/AP Images, 42; Bill Wippert/AP Images, 45

Editor: Patrick Donnelly
Series Designer: Laura Polzin
Content Consultant: Rita Liberti, PhD, Professor of Kinesiology, California State University, East Bay

Publisher's Cataloging-in-Publication Data

Names: Hall, Brian, author.
Title: Pioneers in women's sports / by Brian Hall.
Description: Minneapolis, MN : Abdo Publishing, 2018. | Series: Women in sports | Includes bibliographical references and index.
Identifiers: LCCN 2017930235 | ISBN 9781532111563 (lib. bdg.) | ISBN 9781680789416 (ebook)
Subjects: LCSH: Athletes--Juvenile literature. | Women athletes--Juvenile literature.
Classification: DDC 796--dc23
LC record available at http://lccn.loc.gov/2017930235

TABLE OF CONTENTS

CHAPTER 1
FROM BABE TO MO'NE 4

CHAPTER 2
COURTING SUCCESS 10

CHAPTER 3
PLAYING HARDBALL 18

CHAPTER 4
THE NEED FOR SPEED 26

CHAPTER 5
HOOPS HEROES 32

CHAPTER 6
OPENING OTHER DOORS 40

GLOSSARY 46
FOR MORE INFORMATION 47
INDEX 48
ABOUT THE AUTHOR 48

CHAPTER 1

FROM BABE TO MO'NE

The picture on the cover of *Sports Illustrated* is much like any other. A pitcher, mid-windup, is about to unleash a blazing fastball. The headline simply reads, "Mo'ne" with the subtitle "Remember her name."

Mo'ne Davis, at 13 years old, was the first Little League baseball player to ever be featured on the cover of the popular sports magazine.

And Mo'ne is a girl.

Boys and girls of all ages saw her picture staring back at them at local newsstands or grocery store checkouts. In 2014 Mo'ne became a household name.

Successful female athletes are seen everywhere today. Serena Williams on the tennis court, Ronda Rousey in mixed martial arts (MMA), and the 2015 Women's World Cup–champion US soccer team are role models for many young athletes today.

Mo'ne Davis autographs a copy of her *Sports Illustrated* cover.

EXCLUSIVE
KOBE IN CHINA
KOBE IN TWILIGHT
BY CHRIS BALLARD
The 13-year-old from South Philly has owned the sports conversation since her shutout of Tennessee last Friday.
Mid-Atlantic
Moné

Lottie Dod, *left*, competes in archery at the 1908 Olympics in London.

The pioneers in women's sports created the opportunity for today's athletes to be successful.

Two female athletes in particular led the way for women in sports. Charlotte "Lottie" Dod and Mildred "Babe" Didrikson were excelling in athletic feats even

ANNIKA SÖRENSTAM

Annika Sörenstam became the first woman to follow in Didrikson Zaharias's footsteps when she competed in the Professional Golfers' Association (PGA) Tour's 2003 Colonial Invitational. Didrikson Zaharias had competed in the 1945 Los Angeles Open. Sörenstam followed Didrikson Zaharias in other ways. The Swedish golf star was named the Associated Press Female Athlete of the Year in 2003, 2004, and 2005. Didrikson Zaharias is the only other golfer to win the honor three years in a row.

before women had many rights. Dod and Didrikson were athletic and versatile.

Dod first made her mark in tennis. In 1887, at age 15, she won the Wimbledon's Ladies Singles championship. She later became the British National Golf champion and won a silver medal in archery in the 1908 Olympic Games.

Didrikson followed Dod's footsteps. She played baseball and basketball growing up but gained worldwide fame as a US Olympic track star. In 1932 she won gold medals in the javelin throw and 80-meter hurdles. She added a silver medal in the high jump.

Gertrude Ederle became the first woman, and only the fifth person ever, to swim across the English Channel. Ederle was just 19 years old in 1926 when she completed the 21-mile (34-km) journey from France to England in 14 hours, 31 minutes. Her time broke the previous record by more than 2 hours.

Didrikson, who changed her name after marrying professional wrestler George Zaharias, later turned her attention to golf. Didrikson Zaharias competed against men in PGA events and became the first woman to make the cut in one. Along with promoter Fred Corcoran and fellow golfer Patty Berg, Didrikson Zaharias founded the Ladies Professional Golf Association (LPGA).

The Associated Press named Didrikson Zaharias the greatest female athlete of the first half of the 20th century. She and Dod were among the first to introduce the world to the athletic potential of women. In many ways, these pioneers and so many others set the bar for athletes such as Mo'ne, who took advantage of opportunities they created for women in sports.

Babe Didrikson pitches for a minor league baseball team in a spring training game in 1934.

CHAPTER 2

COURTING SUCCESS

Early in the 20th century, many female athletes excelled on the tennis court. In 1905, May Sutton became the first American woman to win the singles title at Wimbledon. She did it again two years later. Helen Wills Moody won four straight Wimbledon titles beginning in 1927. But the sport changed forever when Althea Gibson broke through in the 1950s.

Jackie Robinson was revered for breaking the Major League Baseball color barrier in 1947. Three years later, Gibson became the first to integrate the world of tennis. She was the first black woman to compete at the US National Championships, which is now called the US Open. Gibson won five major tournaments, including Wimbledon and the US Open twice, and she took home six more major titles in doubles play. When her tennis career was over, Gibson decided to focus on golf. In 1964 she became the first person of color to play on the LPGA tour.

Althea Gibson returns a shot in a 1957 match at Wimbledon.

Women's professional tennis was largely dominated by Margaret Court after Gibson left the sport. Court won a record 24 major singles titles, the most by any man or woman in history through 2016. Court also won 19 major championships in doubles and 21 more in mixed doubles. She is the only player in history, male or female, to win multiple Grand Slam titles in all three categories.

Billie Jean King established herself as the next women's tennis star in the late 1960s. King won nine major singles titles between 1966 and 1975. But she's perhaps better known for her activism off the court. King was a fierce advocate for women's equality, especially in the sports world. She'll forever be linked to Bobby Riggs and a match called the "Battle of the Sexes."

Riggs was a top player on the men's tennis tour in the 1930s and '40s. But in the early 1970s he was an outspoken critic of women's tennis. In 1973 he boasted that even at age 55 he could beat King, who was 29 years old and at the height of her stardom. King accepted his challenge, and the two squared off before 30,000 people at the Houston Astrodome and a massive worldwide television audience. With $100,000 in prize money on the line, King cruised to a 6–4, 6–3, 6–3 victory.

Margaret Court competes at Wimbledon in 1970.

Equal prize money for women was one of King's top causes. Over the years, King began to notice that the male champions earned much more than the female champions at most tournaments. In winning the 1972 US Open singles title, she earned $15,000 less than the men's winner, Ilie Năstase. King vowed she wouldn't play the following year if the prize money wasn't equal. The next year, the US Open became the first of the four majors to award the same prize money to the men's and women's champions.

Two other tennis greats, Chris Evert and Martina Navratilova, played each other 80 times and met in the singles final of a major 14 times. Navratilova held a slim 43–37 edge in the competition and was 10–4 in major finals against her rival.

King also was responsible for starting the Women's Tennis Association (WTA) Tour. In 1970 she and eight other top women's players boycotted a series of tournaments over the prize money issue. More players joined the so-called "Original 9" and by 1973 the WTA was born. The WTA quickly established itself as the top women's professional tennis organization in the world.

Billie Jean King raises the winner's trophy after beating Chris Evert in the finals at Wimbledon in 1973.

SERENA WILLIAMS

Serena Williams is following in the footsteps of these tennis giants. Williams became the first black woman since Gibson to win a major singles title when she won the 1999 US Open. Williams won the 2017 Australian Open, giving her 23 career major singles titles, second only to Court's 24. Williams is only the third player of either gender to have owned all four major singles titles at the same time twice in her career.

King finished her career with 39 major titles. Only Court with 62 and Martina Navratilova with 59 have won more among women. King was awarded the Presidential Medal of Freedom in 2009 for her contributions to the sports world.

Serena Williams attacks the net in the 2017 Australian Open final.

CHAPTER 3

PLAYING HARDBALL

Althea Gibson was known as the "female Jackie Robinson," but plenty of women have left their mark on Robinson's sport of baseball. Women competed with men in professional leagues at least as far back as 1898. That's when Lizzie Arlington made her debut.

Arlington pitched in a regulation minor league game for the Reading (Pennsylvania) Coal Heavers against Allenton. Arlington's performances were written about in newspapers at the time. However, her professional career ended after just one inning.

One of the most heralded feats on the baseball diamond occurred in 1931. The Chattanooga (Tennessee) Lookouts minor league team signed 17-year-old pitcher Jackie Mitchell in advance of an exhibition game against the New York Yankees. The left-hander entered the game in relief to face the Yankees' two left-handed sluggers, Babe Ruth and Lou Gehrig. Few could have expected what happened next.

The movie *A League of Their Own* put the spotlight on the role of women in baseball.

R

Lou Gehrig, *left*, and Babe Ruth watch Jackie Mitchell warming up.

Ruth swung and missed at two pitches from Mitchell. He watched another pitch get called for the third strike and threw his bat down after he was called out. Gehrig followed with another strikeout. Mitchell walked the next

batter and was taken out of the game, but the teenager had struck out two of the most famous baseball players of all time.

Some have questioned whether Mitchell's feat was legitimate. Did Ruth and Gehrig strike out on purpose to put on a show for the fans? The two Hall of Famers never admitted to faking the event.

In 1953 Toni Stone became the first woman to play in the Negro Leagues. Stone grew up in St. Paul, Minnesota, playing against boys and men. After playing for a series of teams in the Negro minor leagues, Stone signed with the Indianapolis Clowns of the Negro American League. She played the rest of the season as one of the Clowns' top infielders.

Women were provided with an unexpected chance to play ball in the 1940s. Many Major League Baseball players

MANON RHEAUME

Many women got their start in professional baseball by getting a chance to play in the minor leagues. Manon Rheaume became the first woman to play in a National Hockey League (NHL) game when she played goalie for the Tampa Bay Lightning in a 1992 exhibition game. She played professionally against men in the minor leagues and played another exhibition game for Tampa Bay in 1993.

Toni Stone played shortstop for the Indianapolis Clowns in the 1950s.

Ila Borders pitches for the Duluth Dukes in the independent Northern League in 1997.

signed up to fight in World War II (1939–1945). Chicago Cubs owner Philip Wrigley tried to find ways to attract crowds to baseball parks. He put his money behind the idea of a women's professional league. The All-American Girls Professional Baseball League (AAGPBL) began play in 1943 and lasted until 1954.

The AAGPBL peaked with 11 teams in 1950. The league gave more than 600 women an opportunity to play professional baseball. Star players in the AAGPBL included Dorothy Schroeder, Dottie Kamenshek, and Joanne Weaver. They didn't receive much media attention at the time. But in 1992 a fictionalized version of the league's story was told in the movie *A League of Their Own* starring Geena Davis, Madonna, and Tom Hanks. Surviving AAGPBL players were celebrated at screenings of the movie and shared their stories with a new generation of baseball fans.

Effa Manley and her husband, Abe, owned the Newark Eagles of the Negro National League. Effa ran the business side of the team and signed numerous future Hall of Fame players. In 2006 she became the first woman inducted into the National Baseball Hall of Fame.

Pitcher Ila Borders made headlines in 1997 when she played minor league baseball in an independent league. The left-handed Borders had played college baseball for two small schools in California. She made her professional debut with the St. Paul (Minnesota) Saints in the Northern League. She pitched four seasons in two independent leagues, and in 1998 became the first woman to record a pitching victory in a professional men's league when her Duluth Dukes beat the Sioux Falls Canaries 3–1.

CHAPTER

4

THE NEED FOR SPEED

Police escorted 20-year-old Diane Crump to the racetrack through a crowd of spectators openly booing her. In 1969 Crump became the first female jockey in a pari-mutuel race when she rode Bridle 'n Bit at Florida's Hialeah Race Track.

Crump's opportunity to race wasn't welcomed by all. The chaos at Hialeah that day necessitated her police escort. Crump rode Bridle 'n Bit to a ninth-place finish out of 12 horses. Two weeks later, she won her first professional race. A year later, she became the first female jockey to race in the Kentucky Derby aboard Fathom.

Julie Krone followed in Crump's footsteps. She became the first woman to win a Triple Crown race when she won the Belmont Stakes in 1993 aboard Colonial Affair. She later became the first female jockey to win a Breeders' Cup race in 2003 when she rode Halfbridled. Krone became the first woman to win 3,500 races and was the first woman

Diane Crump and Bridle 'n Bit race at Hialeah Race Track in 1969.

Sun drop
OD YEAR
ryan

inducted into the National Museum of Racing and Hall of Fame in 2000.

Shirley Muldowney and Janet Guthrie became pioneers in a different type of racing. The women took different paths to break barriers in their sport.

Lindsey Vonn is one of the fastest women on the slopes. She leads all women with 76 World Cup wins through 2016. She won the gold medal in the women's downhill at the 2010 Winter Olympics, and she holds five World Championship medals.

Muldowney shook up the world of drag racing. In 1965 she became the first woman to compete in the supercharged gasoline dragster competition of the National Hot Rod Association (NHRA). Muldowney switched to funny cars in 1971. She was the first woman to compete in the top fuel cars division. In 1976 Muldowney became the first woman to win an NHRA race. She finally retired from the track in 2003.

Guthrie competed at the top level in both stock cars and open-wheel racing. Her breakthrough year was 1977. That year Guthrie became the first woman to qualify for and compete in the Daytona 500. Three months

Janet Guthrie celebrates after qualifying for the World 600 stock car race in 1976.

FORCE FAMILY

Shirley Muldowney opened the door for women in the drag racing world. The Force family took it to another level. John Force was a 15-time NHRA funny car champion. The next generation of drivers in his family includes his three daughters. Brittany Force is a top fuel driver. Courtney Force races funny cars. Ashley Force was the first woman to compete in an NHRA funny car race.

later, she was the first woman to do the same at the Indianapolis 500.

Perhaps no female driver has become as famous as Danica Patrick. Like Guthrie, Patrick has driven stock cars and open-wheel racers. In 2005 she became the first woman to lead a lap at the Indianapolis 500. Patrick also set Indy 500 records for female drivers with the best starting position (fourth) and finish (also fourth).

In her NASCAR career, Patrick made headlines in 2013 when she won the pole position at the Daytona 500. She was the first woman to ever clinch a pole in a Cup Series race. Guthrie held the previous best starting position of ninth.

Danica Patrick had success in stock cars and open-wheel racers.

ARGENT
HONDA
sparco
bea
meijer
INDYCAR SERIES
ARGENT MORTGAGE
Coca-Cola
TIMKEN
Run-Rite
sparco
Danica Patrick

CHAPTER 5

HOOPS HEROES

Perhaps no sport has meant more to the advancement of women's athletics than basketball. Steady progress made over the years led to the creation of the Women's National Basketball Association (WNBA) in 1997. It's the longest-running professional league in the history of women's team sports.

Women began playing organized basketball when the game was invented in the late 1800s. Soon there were nearly as many women's college teams as there were men's teams. But an effort to prevent women from competing in team sports soon took hold across the country. Some people believed basketball was simply too rough for women to play. Because of this, women's basketball basically disappeared for decades.

The movement was reborn in the early 1970s, thanks in part to the US government passing a law called Title IX. It required colleges and universities to give women the same opportunities as men. That jump-started women's sports on college campuses, and basketball grew the fastest. By 1976 a women's basketball tournament was

Lisa Leslie, *left*, battles for position against Rebecca Lobo in the first-ever WNBA game on June 21, 1997.

SPARKS
9
50

added to the Summer Olympics. Ann Meyers led Team USA to a silver medal that year. She was a pioneer in the sport in many ways.

Meyers was the first female athlete to earn a four-year athletic scholarship when she signed to play basketball at the University of California, Los Angeles (UCLA). She later became the first woman to sign a contract with a National Basketball Association (NBA) team. Meyers participated in the Indiana Pacers' preseason camp in 1979.

Nancy Lieberman was another member of the 1976 US women's Olympic basketball team. Lieberman participated in the Olympics as an 18-year-old before attending Old Dominion University, where she led the Monarchs to two national titles. She also was the first two-time winner of the Wade Award, given to the top female college basketball player in the country.

Lieberman played in a short-lived women's professional league in the early 1980s. Then she became the first woman to play in a men's professional league when she spent 1986 and 1987 in the United States Basketball League, a minor league for NBA hopefuls.

Ann Meyers drives for a UCLA basket in 1977.

NCAA
COLLEGE GYMNASTIC CHAMPIONS
1971
CAL STATE FULLERTON
NATIONAL COLLEGIATE ATHLETIC ASSOCIATION
15

Nancy Lieberman was one of Team USA's first female basketball stars.

Lieberman came out of retirement at age 39 when the WNBA began play in 1997. She played one season with the Phoenix Mercury, then retired to become a head coach and general manager in the league. In 2009 Lieberman was the first female head coach of a men's professional team when she coached the Dallas Legends of NBA's development league. Lieberman was inducted into the Naismith Memorial Basketball Hall of Fame and became an NBA assistant coach with the Sacramento Kings in 2015.

PAT SUMMITT

No woman became more synonymous with basketball than Pat Summitt. An All-America player at the University of Tennessee-Martin, Summitt also won a silver medal with Team USA in the first Olympic women's basketball competition. As a coach she led the University of Tennessee Lady Volunteers to 31 consecutive National Collegiate Athletic Association (NCAA) tournament appearances. Her teams won eight NCAA championships and competed in 13 NCAA title games. Summitt retired in 2012 with 1,098 wins, more than any coach in women's college basketball history at the time. Summitt entered the Naismith Memorial Basketball Hall of Fame in 2000, and was given the Presidential Medal of Freedom by President Barack Obama in 2012.

Former Kansas star Lynette Woodard is the all-time leading scorer in college women's basketball with 3,649 points. Woodard was a two-time Olympian and captain of the US team that won gold in 1984. She also was the first female member of the famed Harlem Globetrotters.

Lieberman wasn't the first female coach in the NBA, though. Becky Hammon earned that distinction in 2014 with the San Antonio Spurs. Hammon was an accomplished player in college, international competition, and the WNBA. Injuries ended her playing career, but she's proven herself in coaching. Hammon led San Antonio's team in the NBA's summer league and was the first woman to be part of an NBA All-Star coaching staff.

The coaching opportunities for Lieberman and Hammon were aided by the creation of the WNBA. The US women's basketball team got the ball rolling when it won Olympic gold before the home fans in Atlanta in 1996. Capitalizing on that momentum, the league started play in 1997. Team USA stars Lisa Leslie, Rebecca Lobo, and Sheryl Swoopes were among the early faces of the WNBA.

Becky Hammon became a fixture on the sidelines for the San Antonio Spurs.

CHAPTER 6

OPENING OTHER DOORS

Women have been making progress on fields and courts for years. But it's only been recently that opportunities to fill other roles in sports have emerged. Violet Palmer became the first woman to officiate an NBA game in 1997. Dee Kantner was a rookie NBA referee the same year. Palmer continued as an NBA referee for 18 seasons and 919 games before knee problems forced her to retire. Kantner moved on to college and WNBA games in 2002. Lauren Holtkamp became the NBA's third fulltime female referee in 2014.

The National Football League (NFL) has also started to use female officials. In 2016 Sarah Thomas became the first regular member of an NFL officiating crew. Thomas started her journey to the most popular league in the United States by officiating high school games. In 2007 she became the first woman to officiate a major college football game, and two years later she was the first woman to officiate a bowl game. She joined NFL referee Pete Morelli's crew as a line judge in 2015.

Rookie NBA referee Violet Palmer explains a call to Michael Jordan in 1997.

JORDAN
23

NFL
NFL

RONDA ROUSEY

Ronda Rousey is one of the most recognizable female athletes of her time. She won a bronze medal in the judo competition at the 2008 Summer Olympics. Then she turned her attention to mixed martial arts and the Ultimate Fighting Championship (UFC). Rousey's bouts became as eagerly anticipated as those of the UFC's biggest male stars. The former women's bantamweight champion successfully defended her title six times and was named the world's most dominant athlete by *Sports Illustrated* in a 2015 cover story.

Women have taken advantage of other opportunities in football, too. Ashley Martin became the first woman to play and score in an NCAA college football game. Martin was a kicker for Jacksonville State University and a member of the school's women's soccer team. She made three extra-point kicks in a 72–10 victory over Cumberland on August 30, 2001.

Jennifer Welter went one step further. Welter played running back in the Indoor Football League in 2014. The next year she coached in the same league, which opened the door for her chance in the NFL. In 2015 the Arizona

Line judge Sarah Thomas works an NFL game in Arizona in 2016.

Augusta National Golf Club is the site of the PGA's Masters Tournament. It also barred women from becoming members until 2012. Former US Secretary of State Condoleezza Rice and business executive Darla Moore became the first female members of the club.

Cardinals hired Welter as a coaching intern. She helped coach the team's linebackers during the preseason.

Welter's breakthrough was a major story, but she didn't find a permanent home in the NFL. However, Kathryn Smith did. Smith became the league's first full-time female assistant coach in 2016 when the Buffalo Bills made her the special teams quality control coach. It was part of a busy year for female coaching breakthroughs. Dawn Braid became the first full-time female assistant coach in the NHL that same year with the Arizona Coyotes.

The breakthroughs made by women over the years have provided opportunities that the pioneers could have never imagined. They opened doors for today's stars to prove every day that women deserve a place on the athletic fields, courts, rinks, and rings.

Kathryn Smith, *right*, gives instructions to two Buffalo Bills players at the team's training camp in 2016.

BILLS
TRAINI

GLOSSARY

AMBASSADOR

A person who represents a group in the public eye.

DRAG RACING

A type of automobile race in which two cars compete against each other on a short, straight track.

FUNNY CARS

A class of modified drag racers.

HERALDED

Celebrated or given positive attention.

INDEPENDENT LEAGUE

A baseball league whose teams are not affiliated with any MLB club.

LEGITIMATE

Conforming to laws or standards.

MAKE THE CUT

In golf, to post the required score in order to qualify for the final rounds of a tournament.

OPEN-WHEEL RACER

A car with the wheels outside the vehicle's main body.

PARI-MUTUEL

A form of gambling in which those who bet on the top three finishers of a race share the total pool of money bet on that race.

POLE POSITION

The most favorable position at the start of an auto race, typically in the inside of the front row.

STOCK CAR

A vehicle that has not been modified beyond its factory configuration.

SYNONYMOUS

Showing features or meanings that are similar or alike.

FOR MORE INFORMATION

BOOKS

Ignotofsky, Rachel. *Women in Sports: 50 Fearless Athletes Who Played to Win*. New York: Ten Speed Press, 2017.

Kawa, Katie. *Women in Sports*. New York: PowerKids Press, 2016.

Macy, Sue. *Basketball Belles: How Two Teams and One Scrappy Player Put Women's Hoops on the Map*. New York: Holiday House, 2011.

WEBSITES

To learn more about women in sports, visit **abdobooklinks.com**. These links are routinely monitored and updated to provide the most current information available.

PLACE TO VISIT

Naismith Memorial Basketball Hall of Fame
1000 Hall of Fame Avenue
Springfield, Massachusetts 01105
1-877-4HOOPLA
hoophall.com
Visit the place where the history of pro and college basketball is honored and remembered. See the plaques and exhibits featuring some of the finest basketball players ever, such as Nancy Lieberman, Lisa Leslie, and Sheryl Swoopes.

INDEX

Arlington, Lizzie, 18

Borders, Ila, 25
Braid, Dawn, 44

Court, Margaret, 12, 16
Crump, Diane, 26

Davis, Geena, 25
Davis, Mo'ne, 4
Didrikson Zaharias, Babe, 6–8
Dod, Lottie, 6–8

Evert, Chris, 15

Force, Ashley, 30
Force, Brittney, 30
Force, Courtney, 30
Force, John, 30

Gehrig, Lou, 18, 20–22
Gibson, Althea, 10, 12, 16, 18
Guthrie, Janet, 29–30

Hammon, Becky, 38
Hanks, Tom, 25

Kamenshek, Dottie, 25
Kantner, Dee, 40
King, Billie Jean, 12, 15–16
Krone, Julie, 26, 29

Leslie, Lisa, 38
Lieberman, Nancy, 34, 37–38
Lobo, Rebecca, 38

Madonna, 25
Martin, Ashley, 43
Meyers, Ann, 34
Mitchell, Jackie, 18, 20–22
Moore, Darla, 44
Morelli, Pete, 40
Muldowney, Shirley, 29, 30

Năstase, Ilie, 15
Navratilova, Martina, 15, 16

Obama, Barack, 37

Palmer, Violet, 40
Patrick, Danica, 30

Rheaume, Manon, 22
Rice, Condoleezza, 44
Riggs, Bobby, 12
Robinson, Jackie, 10, 18
Rousey, Ronda, 4, 43
Ruth, Babe, 18, 20–22

Schroeder, Dorothy, 25
Smith, Kathryn, 44
Sörenstam, Annika, 7
Stone, Toni, 22
Summitt, Pat, 37
Sutton, May, 10
Swoopes, Sheryl, 38

Thomas, Sarah, 40

Weaver, Joanne, 25
Welter, Jennifer, 43
Williams, Serena, 4, 16
Wills Moody, Helen, 10
Woodard, Lynette, 38
Wrigley, Philip, 24

ABOUT THE AUTHOR

Brian Hall is a sports reporter who graduated from the University of Minnesota following a stint in the United States Army. He lives in Minnesota with his wife and two kids.